MW00899173

Draw a slice of the best pizza you have ever seen.

Draw what you think you could see in a jungle at night.

Use a mirror and draw a self portrait.

Draw five different kinds of flowers.

Draw a picture of a dream.

Draw every thing you eat in one day.

Draw a picture of what you think a sunset on the beach looks like.

What do you think should be on a stamp. Draw it.

Draw a cake.

Go outside and draw the clouds you see. Or draw ones you wish you could see!

Draw an animal that doesn't exist.

Draw something you love.

Make a drawing using only two colors.

Think of something that starts with the letter S. Draw your version of that thing.

Draw a troll.

Just doodle.

Draw something you find in a grocery store.
Add eyes and a mouth and make it a character.

Turn on your favorite music. Draw what you think the song looks like.

Draw your favorite superhero.

Draw your favorite movie character.

Fill a page with a drawing of fireworks.

Fill the page with a spiderweb.

Draw your favorite food.

Draw your best friend.

Think of the funniest face you have ever made. Draw it.

Draw an animal taking a bath.

What do you think America's flag should look like? Draw it.

Draw the kind of bug you think could survive in an Arizona desert.

Draw salt and pepper shakers.

Draw an animal taking a human for a walk.

Trace an outline of your hand. Fill up the outline with words or pictures of things you like about yourself.

Fill a page with stripes. Color each stripe a new color or pattern.

Draw a robot.

If you had an imaginary friend, draw what they would look like.

Draw a map of your neighborhood and include all your favorite spots.

Make 5 dots on the page. Now connect your dots and make your shape into something fun!

Draw your favorite candy.

Draw your favorite tv show.

Draw something in your room.

Draw a bubble gum machine full of gumballs.

Draw something you dislike

Draw something pink.

Use your opposite hand and draw a cactus.

Think of a time you felt very happy and try to draw the way you felt.

Fill the whole page with a drawing of your eye.

Split your page in half with a wavy line. Fill the bottom half with sea animals under water.

Draw something tiny.

Make a continuous line drawing. Don't take your marker off the paper once you start.

Draw anything you want.

Draw a dinosaur.

Draw a place you want to go.

Make an outline of your name and fill it with a pattern.

Draw a family picture.

Draw something magical.

Draw an x-ray version of an animal.

Draw something orange.

Draw the ugliest thing you can think of.

Draw the prettiest thing you can think of.

Combine 3 animals to create a completely new animal.

Draw your favorite food.

Draw an instrument.

Draw 8 circles on a page. Make them into faces with a different emotion on each face.

What is your favorite sport? Draw a picture
of you in a uniform.

Think of the words to a song. Try to draw an illustration of the words.

Find a shadow. Put your page underneath it and trace the shadow. Make it into your own creation!

Draw a picture of what you think summer smells like.

Draw everything you would see on a restaurant table.

Draw a salad.

There is an animal living in your bathtub. Draw it.

What is your favorite movie? Draw a poster of it.

Draw a picture of someone who dug from one side of the earth to the other.

Draw something purple.

Draw a candy bar and the wrapper.

Draw an animal playing a musical instrument.

Draw your favorite animal in their home.

Pick out your favorite color and make a
creation with that color.

Stand up and walk 10 steps. Look down. Draw what you see.

Use something to trace an outline onto the page. Now make that into a new character.

Draw something you miss.

Draw your favorite book characters.

Draw a scene from your favorite fairy tale.

Draw what you would look like if you had fur.

Draw a magical creature.

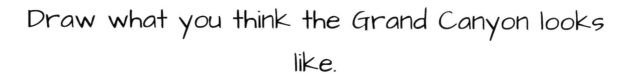

Draw what you think the Grand Canyon looks like.

Imagine you are on an airplane. Look out of the window and what do you see?

Draw anything you want.

Draw a picture of a waterfall.

Draw an apple and a banana talking to eachother.

Draw a comic book character.

Draw your favorite food.

Draw something colorful.

Make up a new hairstyle.

Draw your pet.

Draw something with your eyes closed.

Draw your breakfast.

Draw something from nature.

Draw your dream home.

Draw a pony with a very long tail.

Draw a giraffe eating ice cream.

Draw a pair of shoes.

Draw a happy monster.

62948896R00057

Made in the USA
Columbia, SC
06 July 2019